Rational Emotive
Behavior Therapy

Anxiety and Worry

Revised

Eileen Drilling, M.S.

The following titles compose the complete REBT learning program. Each is available in booklet, workbook, CD's, and DVD format:

Understanding • Anger • Perfectionism
Anxiety and Worry • Depression • Shame
Grief • Guilt • Self-Esteem

Hazelden
Center City, Minnesota 55012-0176

ISBN: 978-1-56838-945-5

The stories in this workbook are composites of many individuals. Any similarity to any one person is purely coincidental.

About the workbook
This workbook is specifically designed for people who struggle with problems of anxiety, worry, and addiction. Drawing on the work of Dr. Albert Ellis and his Rational Emotive Behavior Therapy (REBT), it will show that how we think and behave affects the amount of anxiety and worry we feel. In the pages that follow, we will take part in self-awareness exercises, and we will learn how to alter the self-defeating ways we behave. We will learn how to change our thinking as a way to help us feel and perform better.

Dr. Ellis, who first articulated Rational-Emotive Therapy (RET) in the 1950s, changed the name in the 1990s to Rational Emotive Behavior Therapy (REBT) to more accurately reflect the role behavior plays in gauging changes in thinking. While the therapeutic approach remains the same, the pamphlets, workbooks, audios, and videos in this series have been changed to reflect the updated name.

Introduction

Have you ever felt shaky, restless, jittery, sweaty, unable to relax or stop worrying, and all this without a specific situation or a specific stressor to provoke it? It this happens to you frequently, you may have an anxiety disorder.

Anxiety disorders take various forms—panic disorders, phobias, obsessive-compulsive disorders, post-traumatic stress disorder— each with a specific set of symptoms. A panic disorder can include repeated instances of feeling intense fear often accompanied by chest pain, heart palpitations, or dizziness (but get checked by a medical doctor before you assume this is panic disorder). If you have a phobia, you may have an irrational fear of something specific, such as birds or cats. If you have an obsessive-compulsive disorder, you may experience obsessive thoughts and compulsive behaviors, such as excessive hand washing. Post-traumatic stress disorder often includes flashbacks, intrusive thoughts, and night- mares due to a trauma experienced, such as a car crash. Usually you need professional mental health services when these disorders happen.

But anxiety can also happen as a result of a specific situation or a specific stressor. The symptoms can be distressing but are short- lived. Sometimes people use addictive medications to alleviate the anxiety, or they try to medicate their feelings with alcohol and, over time, become chemically dependent.

Breaking out of the cycle of anxiety and worry

No matter what its source, whether it is a reaction to a specific situation or an anxiety disorder, anxiety can be reduced if we become more aware of the thoughts that accompany it. One method of doing this is to use the REBT process. REBT says that how we think affects how we feel, and how we feel affects how we act.

The *ABC* process described in this workbook is based on the work of Dr. Albert Ellis and his Rational Emotive Behavior Therapy.

The diagram that follows shows how this happens.

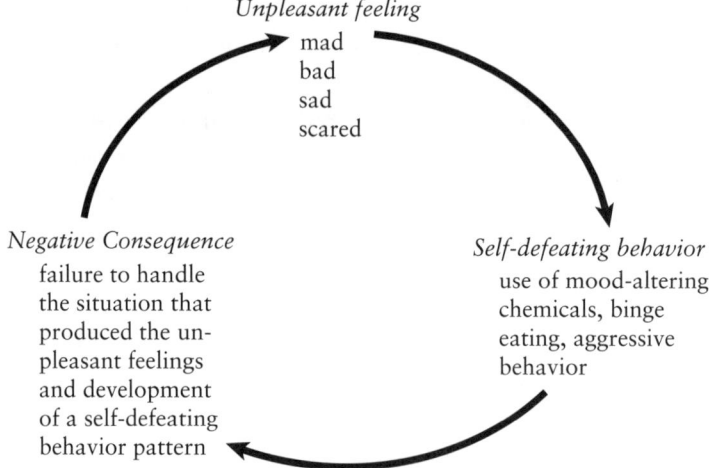

Unpleasant feeling
mad
bad
sad
scared

Negative Consequence
failure to handle
the situation that
produced the un-
pleasant feelings
and development
of a self-defeating
behavior pattern

Self-defeating behavior
use of mood-altering
chemicals, binge
eating, aggressive
behavior

Take a pen or pencil now and write down the self-defeating
ways you behave when you get upset.

_____

_____

_____

_____

Now let's use the REBT process to look closer at specific
troublesome situations in our lives. First, we identify our thoughts
and beliefs about the situation. Next, we identify our resulting
feelings. Finally, we try to change our irrational thoughts and
beliefs to something more realistic. This is called the *ABCD*
process: *A*: Situation → *B*: Thoughts and beliefs about the situation → *C*: Feelings as a result of those thoughts → *D*: Changed
thoughts or beliefs. Consider the following example:

A: *Situation*
My employer criticizes my work.

B: *Upsetting thoughts or beliefs*
She never liked me. I'm a failure.

C: *Feelings*
Anger, anxiety, discouragement

D: *Changed thoughts or beliefs*
What proof do I have that she doesn't like me? One criticism doesn't make me a failure. I can learn from my mistakes.

In order to reduce your anxiety you will need to become more aware of your own feelings and bodily cues that you are becoming tense. For instance, you might notice that your jaw is clenched or that your arms are folded tightly over your chest.
Do the following exercises:

- Scan your body for signs of tension. Write down the signs here.

  _____

  _____

  _____

- Complete this sentence: The last time I felt really tense was

  _____

  _____

  _____

Try the *ABCD* process using the situation you just described.

A: *Situation.*

  _____

  _____

B: *What upsetting thoughts or beliefs did you have as a result of the situation?*

  _____

  _____

  _____

C: *What feelings did you have as a result of these thoughts?*

_____

_____

_____

_____

D: *What are your changed (more realistic) thoughts or beliefs?*

_____

_____

_____

_____

Our thoughts about a situation are called "self-talk." Certain words in our self-talk can make us more upset, for example, "should," "awful," "terrible." *If I think I should do something, I'll feel guilty if I don't. If I think you should do something, I'll feel angry if you don't.* A better way to think or talk about it would be "I'd prefer it if . . ." rather than "I should . . . " or "You should . . ." If you think a situation is awful, you feel worse than if you tell yourself it's unpleasant or inconvenient. Rewrite these statements, eliminating the *should's* and the *awful's.*

- My children shouldn't be so noisy.

_____

- I should be a better mother.

_____

- How awful that I lost a twenty-dollar bill.

_____

Listen to your self-talk for five minutes. Jot down your thoughts as they come to you.

_____

_____

_____

_____

_____

Underline any negative thoughts that you had. Can you find a pattern to your negative thoughts? Are you "catastrophizing" (using the words *awful*, *terrible*, *horrible*, etc.)? Making assumptions? Mind reading? ("I know she hates me.") Predicting the future? ("Things will never get better.") Minimizing success? Maximizing failure? Generalizing? ("*Everyone* will think I'm stupid.")

Affirming the positives about yourself on a daily basis will help you feel more relaxed and confident. Look at your negative thoughts in the preceding exercise and change them to positive affirmations. For example, change

- "I'm a failure" to "I sometimes fail, but I also can succeed. I'm a *person who fails*, not a *total failure*."
- "I know she hates me" to "Even if she does hate me, I can always accept myself and not put myself down by agreeing with her."

Write down your own affirmations here.

_____

_____

_____

_____

Choose one affirmation each week. Write it on a separate sheet of paper, tape it on your bathroom mirror, and say it often. Imagine feeling and acting the way your affirmation describes you.

"THIS IS THE WORST"

In most situations there are some things you can't change. You have used the *D* (*Changed thoughts or beliefs*) section in the REBT process to change your thinking about these.

In most situations there also may be some things you can change. To discover what these are, let's practice the REBT process. Choose a situation that has caused you to react with anxiety or worry. Watch your self-talk for the words "should" and "awful." Watch for patterns of negative thinking. When you have finished, write down actions you could take to change what you can in the situation.

A: *Situation. (Be careful to include only facts.)*

_____

_____

_____

_____

B: *Upsetting thoughts and beliefs. (What self-talk do you use?)*

_____

_____

_____

C: *Feelings. (How do you feel as a result of your thoughts?)*

_____

_____

_____

_____

D: *Dispute your thoughts or beliefs. (Relax and visualize the positive.)*

_____

_____

_____

_____

Once you have completed the *ABCD* process, write down some actions that will help you change what you can in the situation. (Remember, you can change only yourself.)

_____

_____

_____

_____

Choose the actions that seem the most workable and carry them out. Share your experience with your therapist, a friend, or a group of your peers.

If you found the workbook helpful, continue to use the *ABCD* process to develop new habits of thinking and acting. Remember that practice is important.

The Complete REBT Learning Program
Whether you're learning how to put Rational Emotive Behavior Therapy (REBT) to work in your life or teaching someone how to use it, this program benefits everyone. Comprised of nine booklets, videos, and workbooks, plus an audiocassette album, this program helps every kind of learner through print, sight, and sound.

For the learner . . .
Learn by reading: REBT booklets
- introduce you to the *ABC*'s of REBT
- help you understand your past actions and how you can turn them around

Learn by seeing and hearing: REBT DVD's and CD's
- see yourself through others—in real-life situations
- review the videos and audios whenever and wherever you want

Learn by doing: REBT workbooks
- test yourself on the workbooks' questions
- practice and develop the skill of using REBT in your everyday life

For the clinician . . .
A cognitive approach: REBT booklets
- begin the phase of defining the problem
- meet your educational needs for both individual and group sessions

An emotive response: REBT DVD's and CD's
- provide dramatic vignettes and graphic reminders that reinforce core REBT principles
- facilitate group communication, promoting peer-to-peer learning

A behavioral technique: REBT workbooks
- function as effective assessment and evaluation tool
- provide step-by-step guidelines for client goal-setting and goal achievement

For price and order information, or a free catalog, please call our Telephone Representatives.

HAZELDEN
15251 Pleasant Valley Road • P.O. Box 176
Center City, MN 55012-0176
1-800-328-9000 (Toll-Free U.S. and Canada)
1-651-213-4000 (Outside the U.S. and Canada)
1-651-213-4590 (24-Hour Fax)
www.hazelden.org (World Wide Web on the Internet)